HEBREWS

HEBREWS

FROM SHADOW TO REALITY

10 INTERACTIVE BIBLE STUDIES FOR
SMALL GROUPS AND INDIVIDUALS

JOSHUA NG

matthiasmedia

From Shadow to Reality
Second edition
© Matthias Media 2008

First published 2001

Matthias Media
(St Matthias Press Ltd ACN 067 558 365)
PO Box 225
Kingsford NSW 2032
Australia
Telephone: (02) 9663 1478; international: +61-2-9663-1478
Facsimile: (02) 9663 3265; international: +61-2-9663-3265
Email: info@matthiasmedia.com.au
Internet: www.matthiasmedia.com.au

Matthias Media (USA)
Telephone: 330 953 1702; international: +1-330-953-1702
Facsimile: 330 953 1712; international: +1-330-953-1712
Email: sales@matthiasmedia.com
Internet: www.matthiasmedia.com

ISBN 978 1 921441 30 1

Cover design and typesetting by Lankshear Design.

⟩⟩ CONTENTS

›› HOW TO MAKE THE MOST OF THESE STUDIES

1. What is an Interactive Bible Study?

Interactive Bible Studies are a bit like a guided tour of a famous city. They take you through a particular part of the Bible, helping you to know where to start, pointing out things along the way, suggesting avenues for further exploration, and making sure that you know how to get home. Like any good tour, the real purpose is to allow you to go exploring for yourself—to dive in, have a good look around, and discover for yourself the riches that God's word has in store.

In other words, these studies aim to provide stimulation and input and point you in the right direction, while leaving you to do plenty of the exploration and discovery yourself.

We hope that these studies will stimulate lots of 'interaction'—interaction with the Bible, with the things we've written, with your own current thoughts and attitudes, with other people as you discuss them, and with God as you talk to him about it all.

2. The format

The studies contain five main components:

- sections of text that introduce, inform, summarize and challenge
- numbered questions that help you examine the passage and think through its meaning
- sidebars that provide extra bits of background or optional extra study ideas, especially regarding other relevant parts of the Bible
- 'Implications' sections that help you think about what the passage means for you and your life today
- suggestions for thanksgiving and prayer as you close.

3. How to use these studies on your own

- Before you begin, pray that God would open your eyes to what he is saying in the Bible, and give you the spiritual strength to do something about it.
- Work through the study, reading the text, answering the questions about the Bible passage, and exploring the sidebars as you have time.
- Resist the temptation to skip over the 'Implications' and 'Give thanks and pray' sections at the end. It is important that we not only hear and understand God's word, but respond to it. These closing sections help us do that.
- Take what opportunities you can to talk to others about what you've learnt.

4. How to use these studies in a small group

- Much of the above applies to group study as well. The studies are suitable for structured Bible study or cell groups, as well as for more informal pairs and triplets. Get together with a friend or friends and work through them at your own pace; use them as the basis for regular Bible study with your spouse. You don't need the formal structure of a 'group' to gain maximum benefit.

- For small groups, it is *very useful* if group members can work through the study themselves *before* the group meets. The group discussion can take place comfortably in an hour (depending on how sidetracked you get!) if all the members have done some work in advance.
- The role of the group leader is to direct the course of the discussion and to try to draw the threads together at the end. This will mean a little extra preparation—underlining the sections of text to emphasize and read out loud, working out which questions are worth concentrating on, and being sure of the main thrust of the study. Leaders will also probably want to work out approximately how long they'd like to spend on each part.
- If your group members usually don't work through the study in advance, it's extra important that the leader prepares which parts to concentrate on, and which parts to glide past more quickly. In particular, the leader will need to select which of the 'Implications' to focus on.
- We haven't included an 'answer guide' to the questions in the studies. This is a deliberate move. We want to give you a guided tour of the Bible, not a lecture. There is more than enough in the text we have written and the questions we have asked to point you in what we think is the right direction. The rest is up to you.

5. Bible translation

Previous editions of this Interactive Bible Study have assumed that most readers would be using the New International Version of the Bible. However, since the release of the English Standard Version in 2001, many have switched to the ESV for study purposes. So with this new edition of *From Shadow to Reality*, we have decided to quote from and refer to the ESV text, which we recommend.

OVERVIEW: FROM SHADOW TO REALITY

THE SECOND-CENTURY HERETIC, Marcion, was infamous for deleting the Old Testament from his Bible. To him, the just and vengeful God of the Old Testament bore no relationship at all to the merciful and loving God of the New. The Old Testament had nothing worthwhile to say to Christians, and so Marcion simply got rid of it. He also deleted parts of the New Testament that either quoted or echoed the Old. We can imagine that he would have loved the Bible on computer—it would've made cutting and pasting so much easier!

We might regard Marcion's attitude as crude and mistaken, but many modern Christians are Marcionites in practice. They aren't really sure what to do with the Old Testament, and so they basically ignore it. A 'New Testament with Psalms' is the only Bible they need to carry with them.

1. Have a quick glance through the book of Hebrews. How much of Hebrews do you think would be left after Marcion's scissors had finished their snipping?

2. What can we conclude about the relevance of the Old Testament for Christians, as far as the writer of Hebrews is concerned?

3. How does this compare with your attitude to the Old Testament? Are you a Marcionite in practice? What are your main difficulties in reading the Old Testament?

Shadows and realities

In Hebrews 10:1, the writer explicitly says that the Law of Moses "has but a shadow of the good things to come instead of the true form of these realities". The Law spoke of a sacrificial lamb that would take away sin. This was but a shadow (which couldn't really cleanse us from sin) pointing forward to Jesus, the real lamb who does cleanse us finally from our sin. Throughout these studies, we will see again and again how the Old Testament shadows ▶

THE WHOLE ARGUMENT OF Hebrews is founded on the truth and relevance of the Old Testament for us today. The ancient word of God still speaks (Heb 3:7); it is "living and active, sharper than any two-edged sword" (Heb 4:12). And yet for the writer of Hebrews, the Old Testament is to be read through the glasses of God's further revelation in Jesus Christ. The Old Testament is a pointer to Jesus, and can only be fully understood in his light.

In fact, the key way in which Hebrews applies the Old Testament to us, through Christ, is through the imagery of 'shadow' and 'reality'. People, objects, institutions and events spoken of in the Old Testament are but **the 'shadows'; the 'realities'** are found in Christ.

This movement from shadows to realities forms the foundation and framework on which the book of Hebrews drives home its exhortations and warnings. As we study Hebrews in detail over the following nine studies, we will see that the author uses sections of theology (or doctrine) as the basis for his practical exhortations and encouragement. These exhortations and warnings are no mere asides, but the very purpose of the book. Indeed the whole letter is described as a "word of exhortation" (Heb 13:22); that is, a sermon to be read out, listened to and heeded.

4. Quickly skim through Hebrews and note down where the theological (or doctrinal) sections are; also note down where the exhortation sections are that give encouragement and warning.

Theology/teaching sections	Exhortation sections

point to, and yet are surpassed by, the New Testament realities.

On the stage of God's unfolding plan, the shadow comes on the scene first. Like a scene from a Hitchcock movie, we initially only see the shadow coming around the corner. From its shape and size we know something of what to expect of the figure beyond the shadow. But it is only when the figure finally emerges that we see clearly at last! And often when we see clearly, there is a twist or surprise. So it is with the New Testament realities—they are even greater than the Old Testament shadows might have led us to expect.

As we work our way through Hebrews, we will come back to this pattern of teaching and exhortation. In fact, at the end of each study we will fill in part of a diagram (in the appendix) that will build up an overall picture of the contents of the letter. The diagram links together the Old Testament shadow, the New Testament reality, and the exhortation that the author of Hebrews gives on this basis. (Flip over to the appendix and take a look at the diagram, if you wish.)

Hopefully as you fill in the diagram each time, you will be able to see how the argument of Hebrews unfolds. More than that, we trust that God will speak to you directly through this first century sermon, and the Old Testament on which it is built.

» Implications

• As you skimmed through Hebrews in this overview, what things struck you as strange or difficult to understand?

• What do you think was the main emphasis or point of the book?

» Give thanks and pray

• Give thanks to God that his promises made in the Old Testament aren't shadows any longer, but that we can know the reality in Christ.
• Ask God to help you understand more of his truth as you look at both the Old and New Testaments in the coming studies.

DON'T IGNORE GOD'S FINAL WORD

[HEBREWS 1:1-2:4]

1. Have you ever heard someone say, "Well, I would be prepared to believe in God if he would just show himself to me"? How does such a person usually want God to show himself?

2. If God were an impersonal power—like 'the force' in *Star Wars*—how do you think he might show himself?

Read Hebrews 1:1–4.

3. How did God choose to show himself?

4. God speaks to two different groups of people, at two different times and in two different ways. Fill out the table to show the characteristics of each group:

	Group 1	Group 2
When?		
To whom?		
How?		

THESE ASTOUNDING VERSES summarize the whole sweep of human history. They speak of how the world was created, and how it is sustained to this point. They speak of two decisive eras or periods in history. The first is what we would call the era of the Old Testament, those times "long ago" in which God spoke through prophets "at many times and in many ways" (v. 1).

The second—"these last days"—refers to the final period of history, in which the author of Hebrews is writing, and in which we are still living. In "these last days" God has spoken again, but this time in a unique, decisive and final way through his Son. God did not reveal everything about himself or his plans all at once. He did so progressively, culminating in Jesus.

5. Give some examples of how God spoke "in many ways" in the Old Testament. (To jog your memory you might consider: Num 22:26-31; Deut 4:10-13; Ezek 1:4-28; Dan 5:5-6, 5:22-28, 7:1.)

6. The word translated 'in many ways' carries the idea of something being 'piecemeal' or 'bit by bit'. How is that contrasted with God's word in these last days?

7. Write down everything you can learn from verses 2-3 about the Son. (Some of it is unpacked in great detail in the rest of Hebrews, so don't worry if you can't explain all of it right away.) What do you learn about:

- who he is?

- what status he has?

- what he has done in the past?

- what he still does?

Verse 4 says that the Son is far superior to the angels. This superiority of the Son is then backed up by a series of quotes from the Old Testament—even when God was speaking "long ago" through the prophets, he was pointing forward to the greatness of Jesus.

Read Hebrews 1:5–14.

8. In what ways is the Son far superior to the angels in the following verses?

- Hebrews 1:5-6 (**quoting** Ps 2:7; 2 Sam 7:14; Deut 32:43)

Why are the Old Testament quotes different?
You may like to look up the Old Testament verses in these questions later. You may notice that some of them seem to be different from our English Old Testaments. This is because the writer to the Hebrews was quoting from the Greek translation of the Hebrew Bible, called the 'Septuagint'.

- Hebrews 1:7-12 (**quoting** Pss 104:4, 45:6-7, 102:25-27)

- Hebrews 1:13-14 (**quoting** Ps 110:1)

AS MODERN READERS WE MAY be left a little puzzled by all this talk about angels. Why was it so important for the author to establish that the Son is superior to angels? Some commentators speculate that the original readers of Hebrews were tempted to worship angels, or that they thought that Jesus was just another angel. This may be possible but the speculation is unnecessary. The writer goes on to explain why he has drawn such a contrast between Jesus and the angels.

Read Hebrews 2:14.

9. What was the message "declared by angels"? (See Acts 7:53 and Gal 3:19.)

10. How did God respond when people disobeyed this 'angelic' word? (See, for example, Exod 20:4-5; cf. 32:1-4, 19-28.)

11. What was the message that the writer and readers of Hebrews had heard (v. 1; cf. v. 3)?

12. How did the message come to the writer and readers of the book of Hebrews (v. 3)?

13. Why was it essential to show that the Son was far superior to the angels?

THE PRACTICAL WARNING OF THIS opening section of Hebrews is simple: don't drift away. The image is of a boat which has lost its moorings. Gradually, imperceptibly, possibly without its passenger realizing, it drifts away from the dock. All too soon, it is far out to sea and there is little hope of return.

Unfortunately, this is exactly how some people give up on Jesus. It was a problem for the readers of Hebrews, and it is a problem still. It isn't an overnight decision, but one month follows another, the months become years, and they gradually slip away.

However, as the writer of Hebrews emphasizes, this is not just carelessness or bad luck. It is ignoring the great salvation we have in Christ.

» Implications

(Choose a few of the following questions to help you think through your response to God's word. **Remember** to leave a few minutes at the end to go to the appendix and fill out your summary of Hebrews.)

• How does this chapter's view of Jesus contrast with the way our society usually views him?

• How would you answer a friend who says, "If only God would come and show himself to me, I would believe in him"?

• What are some of the telltale signs that someone is drifting away?

- What are the most common things that cause people to drift away from Jesus?

- Where are the dangers for you?

- **Remember** to go to the appendix and fill in the first section of the diagram for Hebrews 1:1-2:4.

›› Give thanks and pray

- Give thanks to God that the message about Jesus has come down to us.
- Acknowledge to God those areas where you are tempted to drift away and ask him to help you listen to Jesus instead.
- Ask God to help those that you know who are not Christians to understand the significance of missing out on Jesus.

THE MAN WHO RULES THE FUTURE

[HEBREWS 2:5-3:6]

WHAT IS THE FUTURE OF THE human race? Should we be optimistic or pessimistic? In many ways, we have reason to be both.

The last century has witnessed quite extraordinary advances in science and technology. Perhaps we will finally manage to control our world, and live sustainably in it. Yet with the technology have come ecological disasters, two devastating world wars, and genocide on a scale unprecedented in human history.

The last century also experienced great advances in medicine. Antibiotics, bypass surgery, improvements in diet—perhaps we will finally gain control of our bodies. Researchers are predicting that babies born today will routinely live to the age of 120. Yet as we find the cure for one incurable disease, several others seem to pop up. We can save premature babies who otherwise would have died, and we can abort babies who otherwise would have lived. We have cultured viruses for use in vaccines, and also for use in biological warfare.

Will mankind rule the future? What hope is there? Our passage in this study opens with this very issue. Who is it that will rule the world to come? And who is ruling the world now?

Who rules the world?

Read Hebrews 2:5–9.

1. To whom has God subjected the world to come?

Read Psalm 8.

2. Psalm 8 plays an important part in the author's argument in Hebrews 2. How would you summarize its teaching about mankind?

- Man is...

- And yet man is...

3. Come back to Hebrews 2:5–9. As the author ponders Psalm 8, what problem does he see?

4. What is his solution to that problem? What was Psalm 8 foreshadowing or looking forward to?

5. Who rules the world now?

6. Who will rule in the world to come?

THERE ARE SOME BIG IDEAS TO WRAP our minds around in this passage, spanning from the creation of this present world to the glories of the world to come. In the Garden of Eden, everything was subject to man (Gen 1-2). God created mankind to have dominion over the world, and Psalm 8 restates this. At present, however, we do not see everything subject to man. The world is not under our control; it frustrates us and rebels against us. And we ourselves are in slavery because of our fear of death (as Heb 2:14-15 goes on to teach).

According to the writer of Hebrews, Psalm 8 was looking forward to the answer to this dilemma. It was looking forward to Jesus, who became a man and for a little while was made lower than the angels, but has now been crowned with glory and honour through his death and resurrection. He is now the ruler of everything, as man was always meant to be.

If that were not astounding enough, there's even more. Jesus did not become the ruler of all things merely for his own sake. He became lower than the angels for a particular purpose—to bring many sons to glory (2:10). God's purpose was not just that his Son might be the ruler and heir of all things (1:2), but that through Jesus, mankind should come to its rightful place as the ruler of all things.

In other words, Christians are people on a journey to glory. We will one day be crowned with glory and honour, and have all things in subjection to us. On our journey to that world, we have a pioneer; we have someone who has gone ahead of us and blazed a trail (the phrase "founder of salvation" could well be translated "pioneer of salvation", as in some modern versions). Our pioneer has already entered his glory and rule; and he has opened up a way that we can follow.

The perfect pioneer

Read Hebrews 2:10–18.

7. How does the devil hold the power of death over mankind (cf. Gen 3:1-7, 17-19; Rev 12:9-10)?

8. What are some ways in which this might lead to lifelong slavery (v. 15)?

9. In order for Jesus to fulfil his task of bringing many sons to glory, what obstacles did he have to overcome?

10. How was the Son made **perfect** for this task?

11. Why did Jesus have to be a man in order to be the founder or pioneer of our salvation?

12. Whom does Jesus help?

The writer of Hebrews goes on to develop this theme of Jesus as our pioneer, and the journey that we are on, by focusing on another famous biblical journey: the Exodus from Egypt.

Jesus made perfect?

Hebrews 2:10 puzzles many Christians. It seems to suggest that there was a time when the Son was not perfect. The difficulty comes because we usually think of perfection in terms of morality or God-likeness. Was the Son immoral and less than Godlike?! Not only does this clash with our theology but, more importantly, it goes against what we have learnt about the Son in Hebrews 1. The Son is nothing less than "the radiance of the glory of God and the exact imprint of his nature" (1:3), and one who has "loved righteousness and hated wickedness" (1:9).

In what sense, then, was he 'imperfect'? We have been talking about the Son's task as the pioneer who brings many sons to glory. This task involved nothing less than destroying the devil's death grip on mankind, freeing them from slavery to their fear of death. It was for this task that the Son was 'made perfect'. There was a time when he was not able to carry out this role; that is, when he was at the Father's side in eternity. We are used to the idea of people becoming qualified for a particular job. Jesus had to be made perfect—qualified, adequate, complete—for this particular job as the pioneer of salvation. He had to become a man, to become flesh and blood, and to suffer death on a cross.

Jesus is our Moses for the future

Read Hebrews 3:1–6.

13. How is Jesus like Moses, yet far greater (cf. Exod 3:1-10)?

14. Put yourself in the sandals of those who left Egypt under Moses' leadership. What was their hope for the future? Why would they need courage to keep going?

15. What are the implications of the important word "if" in 3:6?

In this study, we have seen that Jesus is the man who rules the future. As the true Adam (the true Man), he is the ruler of the world, both now and in the future. He is the pioneer who leads many sons to their future glory. In fact, he is like a bigger, better Moses who leads us—the true descendants of Abraham—to a bigger, better promised land.

As 3:6 encourages us (and as we will explore further in our next study), all this is a stirring encouragement for us to persevere, and to keep hold of our confidence, our courage and our hope.

» Implications

(Choose a few of the following questions to help you think through your response to God's word. **Remember** to leave a few minutes at the end to go to the appendix and fill out your summary of Hebrews.)

- Are you one of those "sons" who will rule with Jesus? If not, how might you become one? (If you are unsure about how to answer this question, then talk to a Christian friend or check out www.twowaystolive.com.)

- If you are one of those "sons", what will it involve for you to "consider Jesus" (3:1)?

- What things distract you from holding onto your future hope?

- In what sense are we in a far more privileged position than the Israelites in the Exodus?

- How is this a motivation for us to take the encouragement of 3:1 and 3:6 to heart?

- **Remember** to go to the appendix and fill in the diagram for Hebrews 2:5-3:6.

» Give thanks and pray

- Give thanks to God that Jesus has become like us and shared in our world so that we can be rescued from the fear of death and share in his eternal rule.
- Speak to God about the ways in which you are tempted to forget your hope in Jesus, and ask God to help you hold onto your confidence in him.

DON'T MISS OUT

[HEBREWS 3:7–4:13]

WE FINISHED OUR LAST STUDY thinking about Moses, who led the people of Israel out of slavery in Egypt. The Israelites' dramatic escape from the armies of Pharaoh was one of the great victories of the Old Testament. God freed his people from slavery in Egypt through mighty signs and wonders, and this pointed forward to the even greater salvation that God would achieve through Christ—to free his people from slavery to Satan and the fear of death.

However, the Exodus story was not only one of the greatest examples of God's salvation in the Old Testament; it was also one of the greatest tragedies. In the end, the Exodus generation missed out on the blessing of God. In this study we will first investigate what they missed out on and how they missed it, before we turn to the relevance of that for us today.

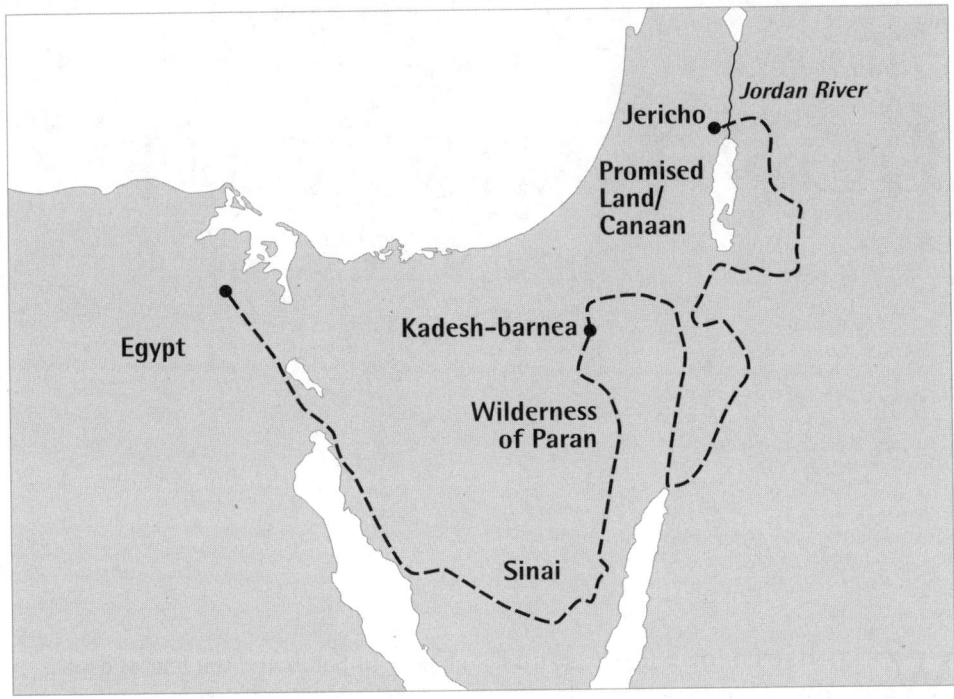

Read Numbers 13:25–14:35.

1. Given the promises that God had made and the amazing things that he had done in the Exodus from Egypt, how should the Israelites have responded to the spies' report at Kadesh?[1]

2. How did they in fact respond?

3. What was God's judgement upon them? What did they miss out on?

Read Hebrews 3:7–4:1.

4. The author of Hebrews quotes Psalm 95 (which itself is about the rebellion of the Israelites against God). According to this quote, and Hebrews 3, what was the real problem with the Israelites?

5. What is our danger as Christians?

6. What are we urged to do about it (in 3:12-13 and 4:1)?

THE REBELLIOUS GENERATION OF Israel missed out on the promised land of Canaan, that beautiful land, flowing with milk and honey. They came so close, right to its southern border. Yet they missed out, because they disobeyed God and failed to trust him. The result was forty years of wandering and death until that whole generation died. As God had sworn in his anger, "They shall not enter my rest"—that is, the land of Canaan, the promised land of God's rest.

Why then does Hebrews go on to say that "while the promise of entering his rest still stands, let us fear lest any of you should seem to have failed to reach it" (Heb 4:1)? Does it mean that Christians should attempt to immigrate to modern day Israel? Should we all be joining tours of the Holy Land led by retired clergy? What exactly is this 'God's rest' that we are to enter?

Read Hebrews 4:1–13.

7. What did God rest from?

8. Thinking back to Genesis 1-3, did humanity ever share in that rest of God? What ultimately stopped them from doing so?

9. How does the author of Hebrews make use of both Genesis 2:1-3 and Psalm 95 to show that there remains a future Sabbath rest for us Christians?

10. What is this future rest? (See also Heb 3:1, 11:13-16; Rev 14:12-13.)

11. In what ways is our experience parallel to that of the Israelites in Moses' time? How ought we to be different from them?

12. What do verses 12-13 say about the place of the Old Testament in our lives?

IN THE FAST-PACED, WORK-OBSESSED world that we live in, it is hard to believe that work might not be the ultimate goal. But it wasn't for God. The creation account of Genesis 1 doesn't finish with God working, but with God resting (Gen 2:1-3). The seventh day of creation was a day of blessing, of rest and goodness.

Adam and Eve shared in it, in the garden that God placed them in. It was a good garden with all manner of trees for food, and rivers flowing from it bringing blessing to the entire world. It was where humanity shared the blessing of good relationship with God as he walked with them in the cool of the day. But humanity lost their share in God's rest when they rebelled against God and were ejected from the Garden.

God set about rescuing humanity through Abraham. Abraham's descendants, the nation of Israel, would once again have the opportunity of sharing in God's rest in the promised land of Canaan, a land of rest and blessing, flowing with milk and honey, a reminder of Eden itself. Once again, however, the promised land eluded them as they rebelled against God in the desert.

It was Moses' successor, Joshua, who led the new generation of Israelites into the promised land. Now at last, surely, they had entered God's rest and were secure! But even while they were in the promised land, King David warned them,

"Today, if you hear his voice, do not harden your hearts" (Ps 95:7-8). The danger was that God would again deny them his rest if they rebelled against him. In other words, if the possibility of missing out on God's rest still existed, there must be some further rest beyond Canaan—ultimately heaven itself (this is the argument of Heb 4:1-10). This ultimate rest was not only in the future for those in David's time; it is still in the future for us.

This is why the author of Hebrews gets so excited about the word "today" from Psalm 95. That word showed him that the danger of hard-heartedness did not end with the Exodus generation, or with David's generation. Indeed, it is an ever-present warning, for every day is called "today". And so Psalm 95 is what the Holy Spirit 'says' (present tense) to us today.

» Implications

(Choose a few of the following questions to help you think through your response to God's word. **Remember** to leave a few minutes at the end to go to the appendix and fill out your summary of Hebrews.)

- What then is to be our attitude towards God's voice, God's word (Heb 4:12-13)?

- How are we to respond to the warning of Ps 95 (Heb 4:11, 3:12-15):
  - individually?

  - corporately?

- How can sin be deceptive? How may sin's deceitfulness harden our hearts?

- Are there particular sins that are especially deceptive and dangerous in causing people in your Christian group to fall away and miss out on entering the final rest of heaven?

- **Remember** to fill in the diagram in the appendix for Hebrews 3:7-4:13. Do you think the writer's exhortations and warnings have become more focused since chapter 2:1-4?

» Give thanks and pray

- Give thanks to God that the goal of creation is not work but rest.
- Ask God to help you work hard at reading his word with a soft heart that wants to hear and obey.

Endnote

1. Also called Kadesh-barnea in other parts of the Old Testament.

CAN A CHRISTIAN FALL AWAY?

[HEBREWS 4:14–6:20]

IF YOU EVER WANT TO SEND SPARKS flying in a Bible discussion group, just raise the question: "Can a Christian fall away?" There will be some who answer "No!" because after all, "Once saved, always saved". They will appeal to Jesus' words that no-one can snatch his sheep from his hand (John 10:28); or to the Apostle Paul's confidence that nothing will be able to separate us from the love of God in Jesus our Lord (Rom 8:39). There will be others who answer "Yes!" because why else would Paul say, "let anyone who thinks that he stands take heed lest he fall" (1 Cor 10:12)? And haven't we all known people who once were with us, but now have 'fallen away'?

Hebrews 6:4-6 has become one of the key passages in this debate. It is often quoted as a proof text for the "Yes" case:

> For it is impossible, in the case of those who have once been enlightened, who have tasted the heavenly gift, and have shared in the Holy Spirit, and have tasted the goodness of the word of God and the powers of the age to come, and then have fallen away, to restore them again to repentance...

Those for the "No" case seek other ways to explain these verses. Perhaps it is merely a hypothetical warning: "...*if* they fall away". Or perhaps the description of having "once been enlightened" doesn't necessarily mean they were really Christians in the first place.

1. What do you think about this issue?

2. Take a quick look at the 'Hebrews overview' diagram in the appendix. What framework might this provide for thinking more about the issue?

The tabernacle

As we will see in more detail in study 7, the tabernacle was the tent that Moses was told to build by God in Exodus 26-27. After it was built, God caused his glory to fill the tent in the sight of all the people as a sign that he now dwelt among them (Exod 40:34-38). The tabernacle was the meeting place where the nation of Israel met with God. It was the site of the sacrifices, the heart of the Day of Atonement ritual (Lev 16) and the symbol of God's presence amongst his people. During the reign of King Solomon, the tabernacle was replaced by the temple, which played exactly the same role for Israel in the promised land. The "inner place" or "the Most Holy Place" (Heb 9:3) was the innermost room of the tent where God 'dwelt' between the wings of the cherubim above the ark of the covenant (Exod 25:10-22).

BEFORE THINKING ANY more about this debate, it is important to remember that the true meaning of any set of verses is heavily determined by the context in which they are located. So let's look at Hebrews 4:14-6:20 to see what the whole section is about, before we return to our vexing question.

In the first four chapters of Hebrews, the author has used the Old Testament context of the Exodus to help us to understand Jesus. The message about Jesus is more important than the law (1:1-2:4), Jesus is a better pioneer than Moses (3:1-6), and he is leading us to heaven, which is far better than the promised land (3:7-4:13).

However, just as the writer has pictured heaven using the Old Testament theme of the promised land, so he now describes heaven as "the inner place", using the Old Testament category of the **tabernacle** (6:19).

With this switch from "promised land" to "inner place", there is also a development in the way the writer wants us to think about Jesus. He is not only the Moses who leads us into the promised land; he is also the high priest who leads us into the inner sanctuary. And so we turn to explore the significance of Jesus' priesthood.

Read Hebrews 4:14–5:10.

3. What similarities can you see between normal human priests and Jesus:

- in their relationship to ordinary people in their weakness?

- in how they got the job?

- in their basic task?

4. What differences can you see between normal human priests and Jesus:

- in regard to their own sin?

- in regard to the priestly order they belong to?

5. In what sense did Jesus have to "learn obedience" and be "made perfect" (5:8-9)? (See also Luke 22:39-46.)

6. What was the result of the Son's willing obedience to his Father?

7. How does Jesus' obedience relate to the confidence that a Christian can have in approaching God (4:14-16; cf. 6:19-20)?

CHARLES WESLEY'S HYMN, 'AND CAN It Be', echoes this confidence and assurance:

> Bold I approach the eternal throne
> And claim the crown through
> Christ my own.

Our journey to heaven is guaranteed because Jesus is our great high priest who has gone into heaven on our behalf. His high priesthood is the basis of our confidence in approaching God. He is the priest—the 'go-between' or mediator— between God and us. Like Aaron, Jesus can adequately represent us because he too was chosen from among men and is able to sympathize with our weaknesses. On the other hand, we also need a 'go-between' who is acceptable to God. God shows that Jesus is that 'go-between' by designating him as a priest in the order of Melchizedek.

The author has more to say about Melchizedek, but he pauses, because he doesn't think his readers have what it takes to understand or accept it (5:11). And as he chides them for their immaturity, he comes to the famous warning about falling away.

Read Hebrews 5:11–6:12.

8. Why didn't the writer think his readers had what it takes to accept the teaching about Jesus and Melchizedek?

9. His solution seems a little strange at first—to move on from the "elementary doctrine" of Christ—but not when we realize that all of these elementary teachings are found in the Old Testament. That is, they are not distinctively Christian teachings, but basic or foundational teachings within Judaism itself.

   Given the overall purpose of the letter, what do you think the author of Hebrews is warning his readers about? What would 'falling away' mean for them?

10. What actually is "impossible" (6:4-6)? What is the main thrust of this warning?

11. How is the warning of 6:7-8 related to the warning of 6:4-6?

12. Which of Jesus' parables does 6:7-8 remind you of?

13. How confident is the writer that his readers will actually go on to maturity? Why?

14. Why do you think he gives such stern warnings?

Read Hebrews 6:13-20.

15. On what basis can we be sure of inheriting the blessing of heaven?

16. How do these verses promote our continual trust in God?

As always in our Bible reading, we must be careful of imposing our questions on the text, rather than listening to the questions that the text actually addresses. The issue that the author of Hebrews addresses is not whether or not we can fall away, but whether or not someone who has fallen away can turn back. And his answer is "No"! It is impossible for them to be brought back to repentance. There is a point of no return.

It is important to notice what 'falling away' actually means. It is not merely what we might call 'backsliding' as a Christian. For these Jewish Christians, who had received God's revelation that Jesus was the Messiah and High Priest, 'falling away' meant reverting to Old Testament religion. To 'fall away' meant falling from the reality back to the shadow. It meant that they would ultimately be rejecting the Messiah, as their first-century Jewish countrymen had done, and thus they would be "crucifying once again the Son of God to their own harm and holding him up to contempt". The exact details of how they would be doing this are spelt out in chapters 7-10.

While they were in danger of falling away, of going past that point of no return, they had not yet gone that far. The writer is confident of better things in their case. Nevertheless, there was real danger, given the direction they were going, and they needed a stern warning. It's rather like telling small children not to play too close to the edge of a cliff, and yet they keep wandering closer and closer. They have not gone over the edge, but the danger is real. One way to warn them is to pick them up and dangle them over the edge so they can have a good look at the drop and the big rocks at the bottom!

It is because these Jewish Christians had not yet gone over the cliff that the warning is possible. Once they go beyond the point of no return, it is too late for warnings. Repentance is not possible.

We can't dilute the warning of this passage by saying that it is only hypothetical; that there is no real danger of them falling away. If that is the case, then the warning makes no sense. If there is a secure, two-metre high, steel fence guarding the edge of the cliff, warnings are not necessary. No, in the mind of the author it is a real possibility and a real danger, and that is why the alert needs to be sounded.

So can a Christian fall away?

We began this study with the contrast between those who think that Christians can fall away, and those who think that they can't. It was a contrast based on the warning passages on the one hand (Heb 6; 1 Cor 10), and the assurance passages on the other (Rom 8; John 10). However, we have found that Hebrews 6 contains both warning and assurance! How can that be? Is the writer contradicting himself? I think not.

The truth is that we have made a mistake in how we have posed the question. "Can a Christian fall away?" is a theoretical question, to be asked and answered in the abstract. The New Testament asks a far more direct and important question: "Will *you* fall away?"

It is a personal question, not some topic for academic discussion. And the answer is, "Make sure you don't!" Both the warning and the assurance push us to the same conclusion: make sure you keep trusting God. The warnings are there to scare us about the consequences if we don't continue to trust him; the assurance passages are there to generate our continual faith, for they speak of a God who is faithful and who can keep us from falling. Either way, the message is simple: keep trusting, maintain your hope, don't give up.

The writer of Hebrews is not interested in theological 'black box' questions as to whether or not Christians can fall away. Rather, he is a pastor at heart and writes pastorally, challenging his readers to make sure they make it to the end. God's promise is sure and Jesus has already entered the inner sanctuary as the high priest on their behalf. To reject the assurance that this high priest brings is folly in the extreme. If only they, and we, properly understood Jesus as that high priest in the order of Melchizedek, then they would come to maturity and be guarded against falling away. And to this we will turn in the next study.

» Implications

(Choose a few of the following questions to help you think through your response to God's word. **Remember** to leave a few minutes at the end to go to the appendix and fill out your summary of Hebrews.)

- Do you think you need such a warning about the direction in which your life is going at present?

- What evidence is there that you are soil that produces a useful crop?

- "Genuine faith is faith that continues to the end." Comment.

- **Remember** to fill in the diagram in the appendix for Hebrews 4:14-6:20. How has our understanding of the readers' situation become more clear since study 1?

» Give thanks and pray

- Give thanks to God that we can have confidence to come to him, not because of ourselves, but because of Jesus' perfect obedience even to the point of death.
- Ask God to help you and those you love to hear the warnings of his word. Pray that God would keep you from rejecting Jesus.

'MEL' WHO?

[HEBREWS 7:1-28]

WHEN CHRISTIANS NAME THEIR babies, you get lots of Joshuas, Benjamins, Hannahs and other fine biblical names, but you don't often meet a Melchizedek.

The intriguing thing about Melchizedek in the Bible is that he doesn't seem to have been given that name by his parents either. According to Hebrews, Melchizedek was someone "without father or mother or genealogy, having neither beginning of days nor end of life" (Heb 7:3). Was he created out of nothing? Did he simply disappear, like Enoch, who "walked with God, and he was not, for God took him" (Gen 5:24)?

While this may be fascinating, many of us might well be asking, "What's the point? Why do I need to study this? Aren't there better ways to use my time?"

We must let the Bible determine our Christian diet, rather than our 'felt needs', because all too often, our felt needs are not our real needs. It's the same with what we eat: my felt need may be for chocolate, but that is not my real need (as my wife is always quick to point out).

What is our real need? We will return to that question at the end of the study. For the moment we need to note that it was crucial for Jesus to be in the order of Melchizedek. If he wasn't, then he could not be the 'fitting' high priest who meets our need (Heb 7:26). Indeed, if he wasn't, he couldn't be a priest at all!

To understand the importance of the Melchizedek argument for the Jewish Christians to whom Hebrews was written, we need to understand their mindset. There were two jobs, or positions, that were vital to the nation of Israel in the Old Testament: that of king, and that of priest. Let's find out about them.

Read Genesis 49:8-10 and Psalm 110:1-3.

1. The king:

   - What tribe did he come from?

   - What was his job?

Read Numbers 3:5-10 and Leviticus 16:6-10.

2. The high priest:

   - What tribe did he come from?

   - What was his job?

3. According to Hebrews so far, which of these positions did Jesus come to fulfil? (See Heb 1:3, 5, 13; 2:17.)

4. Given that we know Jesus was descended from Judah (Matt 1:1-2), why then was it logically impossible for these Jewish Christians to remain Christian? (See also Heb 7:13-14.)

WE ARE USED TO THE FACT that only those from the right family can become king or queen, but in Israel of old, both king and priest needed to be from the right ancestral line. As we have seen above, Jesus was not a descendant in the line of Aaron, nor was he even of the tribe of Levi. How then could Jesus be a high priest at all… unless there was another order, another pattern of priesthood spoken of in the Old Testament? In fact, there was just such an alternative priesthood, mentioned in Psalm 110—the priesthood in the order of **Melchizedek**. Let's take a look at it.

Read Hebrews 7:1-28.

5. From verses 1-10, how is Melchizedek greater than Levi?

Melchizedek

References to Melchizedek are extremely rare in the Bible. The author of Hebrews is the only one in the New Testament to refer to either Psalm 110:4 or Melchizedek. In many places in the New Testament, Jesus is identified as the king spoken of in Psalm 110. But our writer seizes upon Psalm 110:4 as if to say, "Look, this king whom David calls 'Lord' is not just a king, not just the Messiah, but he is a priest as well!"

In the Old Testament, the only reference to Melchizedek, besides Psalm 110:4, is Genesis 14:17-20. These two little Old Testament passages are rare gems for our author, for in viewing both of them he is able to show that Jesus' priesthood is far greater than Aaron's.

6. Now look at verses 11-28. Fill in the following table to see all the differences between the two orders of priesthood.

	Priesthood of Levi/Aaron	Priesthood of Melchizedek
Ancestry; requirement of descent		
Relation to law		
Connection with oath		
Number of priests		
Duration and effectiveness of their work		
Sinfulness of priest		

7. How did Jesus become the high priest "after the order of Melchizedek" (6:15-20)?

8. What is the key achievement of his priesthood? How is Jesus' priesthood far greater than Aaron's?

WHILE THERE ARE CERTAINLY SOME **puzzling details** in this passage, the main point is very clear. Just as David foresaw a greater 'rest' than the promised land of Canaan, and looked forward to it (in Psalm 95, quoted in Hebrews 3-4), so he also envisaged a new and greater priesthood. The Levitical priesthood was still the only functioning priesthood as David penned Psalm 110, yet he speaks not of it, but of God's solemn oath about another priest in the order of Melchizedek. The very fact that this oath came after the law concerning Levitical priests, promising a completely different priesthood, meant that something was inadequate with the Levitical one. Something new and greater was required.

Thus, where the Levitical/Aaronic priests failed to meet our need, Jesus succeeds. He fulfils God's promise of the king who is also the priest, just like Melchizedek. He is the priest-king in the order of Melchizedek. He lives forever, exalted above the heavens, seated at God's right hand, thus holding his priesthood permanently. This is the one who meets our need, who makes a once-for-all sacrifice for sins, who saves eternally those who draw near to God through him.

» Implications

(Choose a few of the following questions to help you think through your response to God's word. **Remember** to leave a few minutes at the end to go to the appendix and fill out your summary of Hebrews.)

- Why is it important for us to understand what it means that Jesus is a high priest in the order of Melchizedek?

Puzzling details

What do we make of the fact that Melchizedek didn't have parents and didn't die? Is he God the Son making some sort of guest appearance in the Old Testament? No, all Hebrews is saying is that Genesis (a book full of genealogies) does not mention Melchizedek's ancestry or death. He comes from nowhere and then disappears from the scene just as mysteriously. The silence over his ancestry and death in Genesis fittingly sets him up as a pattern of the One to come, namely Jesus.

Another perplexing detail is the idea that Levi was "in the loins of his ancestor" Abraham. This is part of the collective thinking of the Old Testament worldview. you are in solidarity with your family clan, including your ancestors. Or putting it the other way, a father contains in his body all his descendants. For us Westerners, the whole idea of genetic connection from one generation to the next may help us understand it. In any case, because of this connection, since Melchizedek is greater than Abraham, he is also greater than Levi.

- Jesus did not come as a social worker, a doctor, an engineer, a philosopher, or even as a sportsman. He came as a high priest. What does this say about the real need of humanity?

- If Jesus meets our need as the high priest in the order of Melchizedek, what need do we have for human 'priests' now? Where do you see the tendency to have human priests as our intercessors and mediators in church life?

- **Remember** to fill in the 'shadow' and 'reality' sections of the diagram in the appendix for Hebrews 7:1-10:25. (Leave room to write more after you've studied chapters 8-10 in our next two studies.)

» Give thanks

- Give thanks to God that he reminds us in his word about our real needs (it is so easy to lose sight of the bigger picture in the details of life).
- Give thanks that he has done something to deal completely with all our sins.

THE OBSOLETOR

[HEBREWS 8:1-9:28]

EVERY NOW AND THEN, SOMETHING comes along that changes the whole landscape. The old ways become outdated, irrelevant and obsolete, sometimes overnight.

One obvious example is the personal computer. Within quite a short time after the arrival of the PC, the typewriter was history—and for a very obvious reason. The PC was simply superior. The new technology made the old obsolete, and no-one would buy a typewriter today unless they were an antique collector.

Nevertheless, there is some connection, some similarity, between the typewriter and the PC. They both have the same aim (producing 'typed' documents). They have the same basic keyboard, with letters and numbers arranged in the same configuration. In fact, we might even say that the typewriter embodied the very function and pattern of a 'writing machine'. It's just that the PC does a far superior job.

That is the kind of relationship in Hebrews between the old and the new. In the Old Testament, God revealed the 'pattern' or the 'shadow' of what was required for sinful people to relate to God. These 'shadows' become obsolete once the perfect 'reality' appears on the scene. The New Testament is all about how Jesus brings the 'superior reality'.

So let's take a quick look at what these Old Testament 'shadows' were, before we see how they have been superseded and transformed by the 'reality' in Jesus.

Read Exodus 24:3-8.

1. What did it mean for the Israelites to be faithful to the covenant given to Moses at Mount Sinai?

2. How was this covenant sealed?

Read Hebrews 9:1-10

3. Hebrews 9:1-10 summarizes the regulations for worship under the old covenant, including what was to happen on the annual Day of Atonement (described in detail in Leviticus 16). On the plan below:

- label the various items mentioned in Hebrews 9:1-10.
- show the activities of the priests and high priest in the tabernacle.

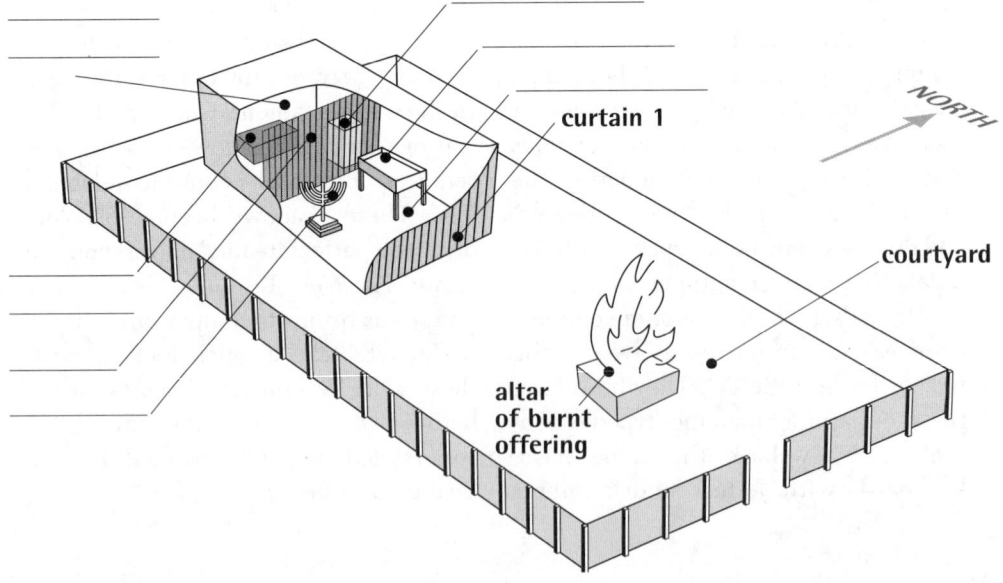

curtain 1

NORTH

courtyard

altar of burnt offering

4. What does the whole set-up of the tabernacle teach us about God, and mankind's relationship with God? What does it teach us about how we can approach God?

Read Hebrews 8:1-13.

5. What was essentially wrong with the "first covenant"?

6. How would the new covenant, promised through Jeremiah, be superior to the old?

Read Hebrews 9:1-28.

7. What does the new covenant achieve that the old never could?

8. How is the priestly ministry of Jesus superior to the ministry of the old covenant priests with regard to:

- where it takes place?

- how often it takes place?

- the nature and quality of the sacrifice?

- what is achieved?

9. Why was blood necessary in both the old and the new covenants?

10. If the Old Testament sacrifices only cleansed the people ceremonially and outwardly, how then are they saved?

11. Imagine you had to explain what 'Jesus died for us' meant to a non-Christian. How would you do it using the categories and ideas of high priest and sacrifice?

As the high priest of the good things that have come, Jesus makes us clean before God by offering himself as the sacrificial lamb. It is by this death, this shedding of blood, that our sins are forgiven and our consciences cleansed.

Notice that what is being talked about is not feelings of guilt, but guilt itself. It is not simply a matter of feeling clean, but actually being clean before God. He is no longer angry at us and our sin, for his anger has been poured out upon the one true sacrificial lamb whose blood was shed on the cross. This high priest has done in reality what the earthly priests could only do symbolically. And because of this he has brought in the new covenant (Heb 9:15). Through him, the 'newness' of the new covenant can now be ours: now we can have God's laws written on our hearts; now we can all know God directly and have immediate access to him—all because God has forgiven our wickedness through the priestly ministry of Jesus. The new has arrived; nothing can be the same again.

As Hebrews 8-9 makes very clear, this was always God's plan. The old covenant was not meant to last forever. It was a forerunner, a shadow, a pattern. It was meant to point to Jesus. And when he came, as the new and great high priest offering the one, sufficient sacrifice for all time, he put an end to all the priestcraft of the old covenant.

He was the Obsoletor.

›› Implications

(Choose a few of the following questions to help you think through your response to God's word. **Remember** to leave a few minutes at the end to go to the appendix and fill out your summary of Hebrews.)

• What do you do when you are weighed down by a guilty conscience? What should you do?

- How can you be sure that you will be saved and admitted into God's presence in heaven?

- How is it that a cleansed conscience will enable us to serve God (Heb 9:14)? How may this be related to having God's laws written on our hearts (Heb 8:10)?

- Are there some church practices that are still locked into the system of the old covenant?

- **Remember** to fill in more of the 'shadow' and 'reality' sections in the appendix for Hebrews 7:1-10:25 (leave room for chapter 10!).

» Give thanks and pray

- Give thanks to God that we no longer need all of the paraphernalia of the Old Testament sacrificial system to come to him.
- Ask God to help you to serve him in some specific areas of your life (cf. Heb 9:14).

THE PRIEST WHO SAT DOWN

[HEBREWS 10:1-25]

1. We have seen over the past two studies that the tabernacle, priests and sacrifices that God had commanded in the first covenant (i.e. the Law) were but a shadow, not the realities themselves. Why did God bother with the shadows at all? Why not just go straight to the reality?

LIKE THE SHADOW OF AN APPROACH-ing giant, the Old Testament shadows function as a visual aid, giving us an idea of what the realities to come would be like. They give us the outline, the shape, the categories of thought by which we understand Jesus and what he did.

In the last study, we looked at the ministry of the high priest on the Day of Atonement (Heb 9:1-10 and Lev 16), and drew out the significance of that visual aid for our understanding of Jesus. In this study, we will not only see that there is more that the Day of Atonement shadow has to teach us, but that important practical consequences follow.

Read Hebrews 10:1–18.

2. How is the inadequacy of the Day of Atonement sacrifices seen in:

- how often they had to be performed?

- the kind of sacrifices made?

- the posture of the high priest?

3. What do you think "make perfect" means in Hebrews 10:1?

4. It was not only the Day of Atonement that testified to the system's inadequacy. The author of Hebrews also quotes and applies a psalm of David (Ps 40) in verses 5–10 to back up his point.

a. How does this quotation demonstrate that the old covenant sacrifices were not God's final solution to human sin?

b. How is Jesus' sacrifice of himself different from the sacrifice of animals?

c. What does it mean to have been "sanctified"/"perfected" through the sacrifice of Jesus' body (10:10, 14)?

Look again at verses 11–18.

5. Previously in Hebrews, we have seen how Psalm 110 was significant in showing Jesus as the priest-king, who reigned with authority at God's right hand. What new significance does the author draw from this psalm (in vv. 11-13)?

6. Why then is Jesus' resurrection and exaltation at God's right hand such a source of assurance for us?

Once for all

In the Law, God required sacrifices and offerings to be made. Yet he was not pleased with them, for they were powerless to do their job. His ultimate plan was to send his Son as a man with a body, and for that body to be offered as a sacrifice for the sins of the world. Yet the Son was not an involuntary sacrifice, being dragged screaming and kicking to the cross. Instead, he came as a Son who willingly obeyed his Father's will. This was the reality to which the shadow sacrifices pointed.

As the author of Hebrews said right at the outset, "After making purification for sins, he sat down at the right hand of the Majesty on high" (Heb 1:3; see also 1:13, 8:1). The posture of our high priest in heaven is the evidence that the perfect, final sacrifice has been made. He is not standing, but has sat down. The task is finished. He is a priest in heaven interceding for us, but not offering a sacrifice for us any more. His present ministry as high priest in heaven is based on his past completed work on the cross. The reality has come, and it does the job once for all time.

7. Look back at all the references to **"once for all"** (9:12, 26-28; 10:2, 10, 14). Why is this phrase so significant?

WE HAVE NOW REACHED THE end of the theological section that spanned from Hebrews 7:1-10:18. The "therefore" of verse 19 signals the practical application of all that has been said in the previous three chapters. But this central theological section of Hebrews has gone for quite some length, and so the writer first gives a quick summary before he drives home his exhortation.

Read Hebrews 10:19–25.

8. How do verses 19-21 (and even verses 22b and 23b) summarize chapters 7-10?

9. What three exhortations then follow? What do they mean?

- "Let us..." (v. 22)

- "Let us..." (v. 23)

- "Let us..." (vv. 24-25)

10. How do these exhortations or encouragements spring from the teaching of the last three chapters?

11. How do these exhortations relate to the future?

The importance of the future

As we think back over our earlier studies in Hebrews, the Christian life has a strong 'future focus'. We are those who will inherit salvation (1:14) and we ignore such a great salvation to our peril (2:1-3). We are the sons (i.e. heirs) whom God is bringing to glory, for Christ is the pioneer of our salvation (2:10). He has got there ahead of us, and we are yet to get there. We are like the Exodus generation, en route to our promised land, our future rest of heaven; but unlike them we are not to harden our hearts, lest we miss out as they did (Heb 3-4). We are not to fall away, but to continue in diligence to the very end so as to inherit what has been promised (6:1-12). We are the heirs who have taken hold of the hope offered to us, a future certainty, firm and secure because Jesus has gone ahead into the inner place, the very presence of God, as a high priest on our behalf (6:18-20).

THROUGHOUT HEBREWS, THE **future** orientation of the Christian life is constantly presented to us. The exhortation in Hebrews 10:22-25 drives this home.

Firstly, we are to "draw near with a true heart in full assurance of faith". The goal of the Christian life is to "draw near" to God: to enter the Most Holy Place, the inner place (6:19), the presence of God (9:24). We "draw near" with a true heart, as opposed to the hardened hearts of the Exodus generation, and with "full assurance" because Christ, our high priest, has already gone before us (6:19-20).

Secondly, to "hold fast the confession of our hope without wavering" looks again to that same future certainty of entering behind the curtain into the inner place (6:18-20). What we profess with our intellect and lips, we are to hold onto in the way we live.

Thirdly, we are not lone individuals as we head towards this hope of heaven, but we are to encourage one another as we see that Day of Jesus' return fast approaching (10:24-25). This care for fellow travellers has already been stressed in Hebrews 3:12-14 and 6:9-10.

Indeed, the rest of the epistle spells out more explicitly what this future-oriented lifestyle is all about. It is worth noting, however, that this future orientation is based on what has already happened in the past—indeed, what has already been accomplished in the past. That is what the theological foundation (Heb 7:1-10:18) has been about: Jesus' finished work on the cross. We have moved from shadows to reality. He is our high priest in heaven who has made the sacrifice once for all time. He is not standing. He has sat down!

» Implications

(Choose a few of the following questions to help you think through your response to God's word. **Remember** to leave a few minutes at the end to go to the appendix and fill out your summary of Hebrews.)

• How central is Christ's finished work in your thinking? How does it affect your thinking about the future?

• Are there any changes you need to make in your life as a result?

• How are you obeying the exhortation of verses 24-25? What obstacles or pressures make it difficult?

- What do you notice is different about the new covenant gathering (described in 10:24-25) when compared with the old covenant one (described throughout chapters 9-10)? How do you think this should be reflected in our church gatherings?

- **Remember** to complete the diagram in the appendix for Hebrews 7:1-10:25.

» Give thanks and pray

- Give thanks to God that all your sins have been completely dealt with. (You might find it helpful to think about specific sins and give thanks to God that Jesus' death brings complete forgiveness for them.)
- Ask God to help you keep thinking about our hope as Christians.
- Ask God to help you encourage your brothers and sisters in Christ to press on towards the day that is drawing near.

NO FAITH, NO FINISH

[HEBREWS 10:26-12:11]

ONCE EVERY FOUR YEARS, THE world stops to watch the fastest, the strongest and the highest. The Olympics is the pinnacle of sporting achievement for any athlete. However, not all events are equally prestigious. Often, it seems, it is the shortest race and the longest race that generate the most interest.

The 100m is a blaze of strength and speed. In contrast, the marathon brings fame for the one who endures, who perseveres, who lasts the distance. And interestingly, it is not only the medal winners that get applauded. Even as the last runner staggers into the stadium, he receives a warm welcome. He has run and finished. Some, of course, fail to finish, and for them there is no applause, no acclaim, and no reward.

The Christian life is more like a marathon than a 100-metre dash. It is about enduring; it is about keeping on going when the going is hard; it is about being determined to finish the race and claim the prize, even when that possibility seems a long way off.

At the close of our last study, we saw how the writer of Hebrews urged his readers to "hold fast the confession of our hope without wavering" and to "consider how to stir up one another… as you see the Day drawing near". In this study, we'll unpack what endurance and perseverance mean, both positively and negatively. We'll look at some of the most heart-warming encouragements in the whole Bible, and also at some of the scariest warnings.

Read Hebrews 10:26–39.

1. What are the consequences of "shrink[ing] back" (v. 39) or "sinning deliberately" (v. 26)?

2. What are the consequences of enduring and remaining faithful?

3. Given the context of Hebrews up to this point, what do you think it means to "sin deliberately" or "shrink back"? (See especially vv. 26 and 39; cf. Heb 9:11–14.)

4. After such a stern warning, how does the Hebrews writer give his readers positive encouragement (vv. 32-34)?

5. How does he encourage them to press on (vv. 35-39)?

LIKE A GOOD ATHLETICS coach, the writer of Hebrews gives his readers both fearful warnings and strong encouragements. He reminds them of what he has already said—that if they turn their back on the new covenant in Christ, they have turned their back on the only sacrifice that can truly cleanse them. They are **"sinning deliberately"** and there is nowhere else to go. There is only the expectation of punishment.

However, the author also reminds his readers of their great track record. Their previous perseverance in the face of suffering and persecution is evidence of their confidence. The coach urges them to keep their eyes focused on the finish line and the reward. The better and lasting possessions are just around the corner. That Day is drawing near (10:25); in "yet a little while" Jesus "will come and will not delay" (10:37).

The marathon runner is nearly finished: the stadium is in sight. He's done the tough stuff. Now is not the time to shrink back, but to continue in his confidence, which will be richly rewarded (10:35).

But just exactly what is this confidence like? What is it confidence in? It is in this context that our writer pens his most famous chapter: the 'heroes of faith'.

Sinning deliberately

Here's an optional question for discussion: if for the original Jewish Christian readers, "sinning deliberately" was largely about going back to Old Testament Judaism with its high priests and sacrifices, what would be the equivalent for us?

Read Hebrews 11:1–40.

6. Fill in the following table:

Heroes of faith	What they hoped for	How they demonstrated their faith	What was the basis of their faith	What they did not see

7. Summarize: How do these Old Testament 'heroes of faith' demonstrate that "faith is the assurance of things hoped for, the conviction of things not seen"?

8. When will these heroes of faith ultimately get what was promised? Why?

As these **heroes** show, faith is about having confidence in God's promises regarding the future, and acting upon them despite present difficulties and temptations. That is why God commended them all. They all knew not only that God existed, but that his promises about the future would come to pass. And so they trusted God and his promises through thick and thin. The next part of the letter turns its attention to the greatest hero of all time.

Read Hebrews 12:1-11.

9. Who is the greatest hero and example of faith? Why?

10. How is he more than just an example of faith (12:2)?

The heroes and us

Interestingly, the heroes of faith are more than just examples for us: they are to be examples with us. For it is only together with us that they receive their reward. In terms of Old Testament 'shadows', some of them received the 'shadow' that was promised (e.g. Joshua, who conquered the promised land); others didn't (e.g. Abraham, who remained an alien in the promised land). But none of them got the real rewards that those shadows pointed forward to: the better country, the city built by God, the heavenly one (11:16). And so, having been "made perfect" with us (cleansed and able to approach God because of Jesus' blood), they now finally receive what was promised. They gather with us around the heavenly Mt Zion, the spirits of righteous men made perfect (12:23).

But these Old Testament heroes are not only examples for us and with us; they are also examples surrounding us. Imagine again you are running the marathon. ▶

You are tired. Your arms are feeble. Your knees are weak. But as you enter the stadium you see all the great marathon runners of the past cheering you on—the heroes you have looked up to since your childhood. Here then is the practical thrust of Hebrews 11: "Therefore, since we are surrounded by so great a cloud of witnesses, let us also lay aside every weight, and sin which clings so closely, and let us run with endurance the race that is set before us" (Heb 12:1).

11. Why is his faith especially noteworthy given the situation the readers had experienced (cf. 10:32-34)?

12. Two popular responses when we go through hardships and persecutions are:

- "God has lost control."
- "God is not for us."

What does this passage say?

13. How would you summarize the nature of the Christian life from this passage?

» Implications

(Choose a few of the following questions to help you think through your response to God's word. **Remember** to leave a few minutes at the end to go to the appendix and fill out your summary of Hebrews.)

- Why do you think people in general are not afraid of God these days?

- Do you think Christians should be afraid of God?

- What are some of the things, though not necessarily sinful in and of themselves, that might hinder you from finishing the race?

- What sin might easily entangle you?

- Pick one of the heroes in Hebrews 11 who would be especially encouraging for you, and explain why.

- Martin Luther's famous hymn 'A Safe Stronghold our God is Still' finishes with these words:

> And though they take our life,
> Goods, honour, children, wife
> Yet is their profit small;
> These things shall vanish all
> The city of God remaineth.

Is this your attitude? How may you 'lose out' in this world's terms as you run the race?

- **Remember** to fill in the summary diagram in the appendix for Hebrews 10:26–12:11.

» Give thanks and pray

- Give thanks to God for the encouragement of so many who have looked forward to the fulfilment of his promises and not given in to present suffering.
- Ask God for the courage to say and do what is right rather than just giving in to comfort or sin.

TRUE WORSHIP

[HEBREWS 12:12–13:25]

1. What words and activities come to mind when someone mentions the word 'worship'?

2. What different kinds of worship are there in the world? Why do you think they are so different?

IF GOD IS GOD AND WE ARE HIS creation then worship must really be about what God wants from us, and not what we want to give God. Thus, idolatry in the Old Testament included not only the worship of false gods, but also the false worship of Yahweh, the true God. The golden calf incident was a classic example.

By making the calf, the Israelites were attempting to worship Yahweh, who had rescued them out of Egypt (see Exod 32:1-6). The attempt, however, was abysmal. Not only was the calf a terrible misrepresentation of what God was like, but the sexual orgy that followed was not at all how God wanted to be worshipped. God was not happy, and his displeasure was rightly vented against those who worshipped falsely. Not all worship is valid, especially in the eyes of God.

Even under the 'Christian' umbrella, different people have differing ways of worshipping God. They arise out of different perceptions of who God is and how he wants us to approach him. We must make sure that our worship is true and acceptable, lest we incur his wrath. As our passage warns us, we should "offer to God acceptable worship, with reverence and awe, for our God is a consuming fire" (Heb 12:28-29).

The overarching theme of the remainder of Hebrews is 'true worship'. There is a central section, in Hebrews 12:18-27, which outlines the basis and framework of how we are to think rightly about 'true worship'. This is sandwiched by two application sections, which spell out just what this true worship should look like in practice (12:12-17 and 12:28-13:21). Let's look at each of these in turn: first the right basis for thinking, then the practical application.

The basis: two mountains

Read Hebrews 12:18-27.

3. Complete the table below, which compares and contrasts the 'shadow' and the 'reality'.

	Shadow	Reality
Mountains		
Warnings		
Shakings		

4. On the 'reality' side of the comparison, which things have already taken place, and which things are still to come?

5. Verse 26 quotes the prophet Haggai. How did Haggai look back to the shadows, as well as forward to the reality (cf. Hag 2:4-9, 20-22)?

SO FAR IN HEBREWS WE HAVE already seen the theme of the Exodus played out (such as in chapters 3 and 4). Hebrews 12 brings another slant to this comparison. The Israelites fled Egypt in order to worship God at Mt Sinai, to gather in assembly around him and hear him speak. In much the same way, we too have been rescued in order to worship God together, to gather around a mountain and hear him speak.

Yet the mountain we have come to for worship is not Mt Sinai, but the heavenly Mt Zion. Once again, the Old Testament experience at Sinai was but a shadow and not the real thing. Indeed, the Old Testament itself confessed to this inadequacy, this time through the prophet Haggai. By saying, "Once more",

Haggai not only looked back to Sinai when God had once shaken the earth, but also looked forward to a time when he would do it once more.

The extraordinary teaching of this passage is that we are already gathered spiritually in the heavenly gathering with all God's people, including those from the Old Testament—"the spirits of the righteous made perfect". Already, we hear his voice warning us about the future judgement, when the earth and the heavens will be shaken, and only what 'cannot be shaken' will remain.

We are to live now in the light of that future. To live for the things which will be destroyed in the 'shaking' is short-sighted. We have things of eternal value to live for: a kingdom that cannot be shaken.

Worship in practice

Since we have come to the heavenly Mt Zion, and to the eternal gathering of God's people around his throne, what should our lives consist of? Answer: true worship. In the rest of this study, let's look at how the author of Hebrews wants us to "offer to God acceptable worship, with reverence and awe".

Read Hebrews 13:1–19.

6. List all the words and phrases in 13:8-16 that use the language of 'Old Testament worship'.

7. Now that we are in the 'reality' rather than the 'shadow', how has worship been transformed?

8. Are Old Testament-style worship practices still acceptable to God? Why or why not?

Responding to God acceptably in worship affects every aspect of life. Let's look at the various practical areas that the author of Hebrews highlights.

Read Hebrews 12:12-17.

9. What does Esau missing out on the inheritance remind you of from earlier in Hebrews? What is the practical warning for us?

Re-read Hebrews 13:1-4.

10. How is this different from what our pagan society thinks of as 'love'?

Look again at Hebrews 13:5-6.

11. How is this attitude to money also very different from our world?

Look at Hebrews 13:7-9 and 13:17-19.

12. What is the role and importance of leadership? What obligations do leaders and congregations have towards each other?

13. How is the prayer that ends this letter (Heb 13:20-21) linked to the idea of pleasing and worshipping God?

14. How does this prayer also capture some of the big themes of the letter?

TRUE WORSHIP IS NOTHING SHORT of pleasing God in all we do. Both our words and our actions can be spoken of as "sacrifices" which we now offer to God (Heb 13:15-16). They are not sin offerings, for Jesus' once-for-all sacrifice was sufficient for that. Nevertheless, they are sacrifices with which God is pleased, for he wants our whole life to be lived in worship of him every minute of the day.

This is because we are already in his presence in the 'heavenly church', gathered with all God's people to worship and please him, just as Israel of old did at Sinai. Like them, we are on our way to inherit the promise—indeed, a better promise, not of this creation, but a heavenly rest, the inner sanctuary, heaven itself, the final inheritance, the city to come, the kingdom of God that will not be shaken!

Hebrews has been a 'short' letter of warnings and encouragements, as the author puts it in 13:22. It warns us against the peril of drifting away, even falling away. It encourages us to keep trusting Jesus and his death and to hang in there in the face of difficulties. How will we respond to this word of exhortation?

» Implications

(Choose a few of the following questions to help you think through your response to God's word. **Note:** In this final study we come to finish off our summary of Hebrews in the appendix. The final set of questions in this 'implications' section encourage us to reflect on what we have learnt over the whole series and not just from this study. It is worth setting aside some time to sit back and see the big picture that God is presenting to us in Hebrews.)

- "Worship is more than what you do on a Sunday morning at church." Comment.

- In view of this study, what specific changes do you need to make in your daily worship of God?

- **Fill in the diagram in the appendix for Hebrews 12:12–13:25.**

- Look back at the introduction to the letter in 1:1-4. How much of the content of the whole letter can you see summarized in this introduction?

- Looking back over your summary diagram (in the appendix), see if you can summarize in a sentence or two the flow of the whole argument of Hebrews.

- Why is 'true worship' an apt way of ending the whole letter?

» Give thanks and pray

- Choose two or three of the big ideas of the letter to the Hebrews and turn them into thanksgiving to God.
- Ask God to help you to make some of the specific changes that you need to make as a result of reading Hebrews.

APPENDIX

Heb 1:1–2:4   Heb 2:5–3:6   Heb 3:7–4:13   Heb 4:14–6:20

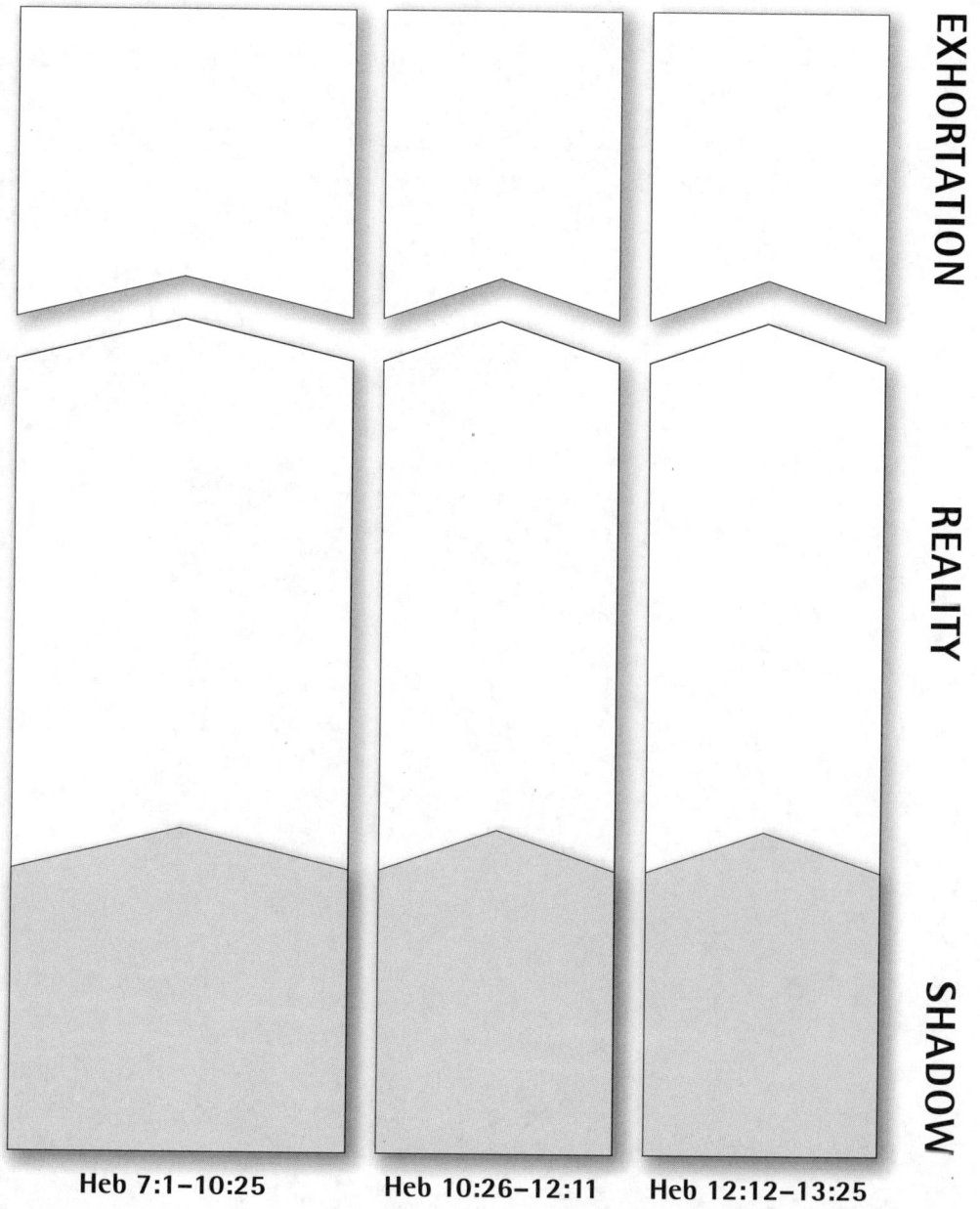

EXHORTATION

REALITY

SHADOW

Heb 7:1–10:25   Heb 10:26–12:11   Heb 12:12–13:25

matthiasmedia

Matthias Media is an evangelical publishing ministry that seeks to persuade all Christians of the truth of God's purposes in Jesus Christ as revealed in the Bible, and equip them with high-quality resources, so that by the work of the Holy Spirit they will:

- abandon their lives to the honour and service of Christ in daily holiness and decision-making
- pray constantly in Christ's name for the fruitfulness and growth of his gospel
- speak the Bible's life-changing word whenever and however they can—in the home, in the world and in the fellowship of his people.

It was in 1988 that we first started pursuing this mission, and in God's kindness we now have more than 300 different ministry resources being used all over the world. These resources range from Bible studies and books through to training courses and audio sermons.

To find out more about our large range of very useful resources, and to access samples and free downloads, visit our website:

www.matthiasmedia.com

How to buy our resources

1. Direct from us over the internet:
   – in the US: www.matthiasmedia.com
   – in Australia and the rest of the world:
     www.matthiasmedia.com.au

2. Direct from us by phone:
   – in the US: 1 866 407 4530
   – in Australia: 1800 814 360
     (Sydney: 9663 1478)
   – international: +61-2-9663-1478

> Register at our website for our **free** regular email update to receive information about the latest new resources, **exclusive special offers**, and free articles to help you grow in your Christian life and ministry.

3. Through a range of outlets in various parts of the world. Visit **www.matthiasmedia.com/contact** for details about recommended retailers in your part of the world, including www.thegoodbook.co.uk in the United Kingdom.

4. Trade enquiries can be addressed to:
   – in the US and Canada: sales@matthiasmedia.com
   – in Australia and the rest of the world: sales@matthiasmedia.com.au

Other Interactive and Topical Bible Studies from Matthias Media

Our Interactive Bible Studies (IBS) and Topical Bible Studies (TBS) are a valuable resource to help you keep feeding from God's word. The IBS series works through passages and books of the Bible; the TBS series pulls together the Bible's teaching on topics such as money or prayer. As at July 2011, the series contains the following titles:

Beyond Eden
GENESIS 1-11
Authors: Phillip Jensen and Tony Payne, 9 studies

Out of Darkness
EXODUS 1-18
Author: Andrew Reid, 8 studies

The Shadow of Glory
EXODUS 19-40
Author: Andrew Reid, 7 studies

The One and Only
DEUTERONOMY
Author: Bryson Smith, 8 studies

The Good, the Bad and the Ugly
JUDGES
Author: Mark Baddeley, 10 studies

Famine and Fortune
RUTH
Authors: Barry Webb and David Höhne, 4 studies

Renovator's Dream
NEHEMIAH
Authors: Phil Campbell and Greg Clarke, 7 studies

The Eye of the Storm
JOB
Author: Bryson Smith, 6 studies

The Beginning of Wisdom
PROVERBS VOLUME 1
Author: Joshua Ng, 7 studies

The Search for Meaning
ECCLESIASTES
Author: Tim McMahon, 9 studies

Two Cities
ISAIAH
Authors: Andrew Reid and Karen Morris, 9 studies

Kingdom of Dreams
DANIEL
Authors: Andrew Reid and Karen Morris, 9 studies

Burning Desire
OBADIAH AND MALACHI
Authors: Phillip Jensen and Richard Pulley, 6 studies

Warning Signs
JONAH
Author: Andrew Reid, 6 studies

On That Day
ZECHARIAH
Author: Tim McMahon, 8 studies

Full of Promise
THE BIG PICTURE OF THE O.T.
Authors: Phil Campbell and Bryson Smith, 8 studies

The Good Living Guide
MATTHEW 5:1-12
Authors: Phillip Jensen and Tony Payne, 9 studies

News of the Hour
MARK
Authors: Peter Bolt and Tony Payne, 10 studies

Proclaiming the Risen Lord
LUKE 24-ACTS 2
Author: Peter Bolt, 6 studies

Mission Unstoppable
ACTS
Author: Bryson Smith, 10 studies

The Free Gift of Life
ROMANS 1-5
Author: Gordon Cheng, 8 studies

The Free Gift of Sonship
ROMANS 6-11
Author: Gordon Cheng, 8 studies

The Freedom of Christian Living
ROMANS 12-16
Author: Gordon Cheng, 7 studies

Free for All
GALATIANS
Authors: Phillip Jensen and Kel Richards, 8 studies

Walk this Way
EPHESIANS
Author: Bryson Smith, 8 studies

Partners for Life
PHILIPPIANS
Author: Tim Thorburn, 8 studies

The Complete Christian
COLOSSIANS
Authors: Phillip Jensen and Tony Payne, 8 studies

To the Householder
1 TIMOTHY
Authors: Phillip Jensen and Greg Clarke, 9 studies

Run the Race
2 TIMOTHY
Author: Bryson Smith, 6 studies

The Path to Godliness
TITUS
Authors: Phillip Jensen and Tony Payne, 7 studies

From Shadow to Reality
HEBREWS
Author: Joshua Ng, 10 studies

The Implanted Word
JAMES
Authors: Phillip Jensen and Kirsten Birkett, 8 studies

Homeward Bound
1 PETER
Authors: Phillip Jensen and Tony Payne, 10 studies

All You Need to Know
2 PETER
Author: Bryson Smith, 6 studies

The Vision Statement
REVELATION
Author: Greg Clarke, 9 studies

Bold I Approach
PRAYER
Author: Tony Payne, 6 studies

Cash Values
MONEY
Author: Tony Payne, 5 studies

Sing for Joy
SINGING IN CHURCH
Author: Nathan Lovell, 6 studies

The Blueprint
DOCTRINE
Authors: Phillip Jensen and Tony Payne, 9 studies

Woman of God
THE BIBLE ON WOMEN
Author: Terry Blowes, 8 studies